THE SUPER COLOSSAL
BOOK OF
HIDDEN PICTURES

Compiled by the Editors of Highlights for Children

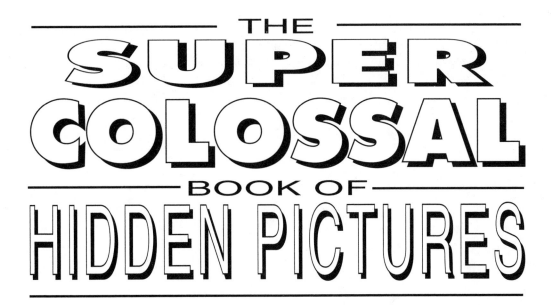

MORE THAN 2,000 OBJECTS TO FIND!

BOYDS MILLS PRESS

Cover

Kool Kats

Making music in the alley with friends is lots of fun. While the Kool Kats jam, you can have fun finding a sewing needle, frying pan, flashlight, shoe, ice-cream pop, rabbit, artist's paintbrush, lady's head, boot, pencil, crown, golf club, ice-cream cone, bird, whistle, and a mallet.

Copyright © 1994 by Boyds Mills Press
All rights reserved

Published by Bell Books
Boyds Mills Press, Inc.
A Highlights Company
815 Church Street
Honesdale, Pennsylvania 18431
Printed in the United States of America

Publisher Cataloging-in-Publication Data
Main entry under title.
The super colossal book of hidden pictures / compiled by the editors of Highlights for Children.—1st ed.
[192]p. : ill. ; cm.
Summary : Each page presents a challenge to find various objects within an illustration.
ISBN 1-56397-362-6
1. Picture puzzles—Juvenile literature. [1. Picture puzzles.] I. *Highlights for Children*. II. Title.
793.73—dc20   1994
Library of Congress Catalog Card Number 93-72920

First edition, 1994
Book designed by Tim Gillner
The text of this book is set in 10-point Clarendon Light.

10 9 8 7 6 5

Quicksand

Billy's big adventure in the rain forest turns into big trouble when he gets in the quicksand. As the monkey tries to help him escape, find a fish, spoon, orange, potato, pencil, snake, turtle, spring, magnet, bird, butter knife, whale, fork, and a feather.

Honey Judge

The Honey Judge is about to give Beth Bear's honey first prize. You'll get a prize if you can find a pot, question mark, trowel, dragonfly, artist's paintbrush, pennant, banana, screwdriver, bell, nail, frog, fish, snail, duck, wrench, candle, crescent moon, shoe, bone, and two butterflies.

Storytime with Dad

Everyone's favorite time of the day is when Dad reads stories. While they have fun listening, you can have fun finding a candy cane, mitten, stocking, butterfly, artist's paintbrush, bird, pliers, sailboat, fish, deer's head, teapot, slipper, and a mouse.

5

Mayan Ball Game

The Mayans are so interested in the ball game that they don't notice the hidden objects around them. See if you can locate a pineapple, lady's head, paper clip, teacup, milk carton, calculator, toothbrush, spoon, scissors, pail, tape dispenser, bird, feather, butterfly, rabbit, ice-cream cone, rose, and a whisk broom.

Donkey Bike Ride

The donkeys leave for an early morning bike ride. While they're away from home, look for a horn, pennant, tack, sailboat, empty spool of thread, pencil, hammer, ice-cream cone, spoon, hairbrush, ladder, candle, and an iron.

If All the World Were Apple Pie

Fishing on the shores of apple pie makes for a good time. You can have a good time, too, finding twelve hidden objects: a pot, turtle, light bulb, snail, wristwatch, mop, ax, cat, mouse, jet plane, screwdriver, and a butterfly.

Dancing Elephants

The monkeys provide the music while the elephants practice their new dance routine. Everyone's so busy, they don't notice all the hidden objects around them. Do you see a fishing pole, dog, seal, peanut, gingerbread man, shovel, fish, ring, lamb's head, mouse, sailboat, snowman, sock, banana, dog's head, top hat, and a carrot?

Three-Legged Race

The kids can't wait to start their three-legged race. As they run, see if you can find a turtle, saltshaker, jump rope, artist's paintbrush, sailboat, toothbrush, hat, carrot, fish, butterfly, bird, hammer, and a lizard.

Collared Lizard

It's hard to see a collared lizard in its southwestern habitat. And it's just as hard to see the hidden objects around it. Try to find a kite, sock, mitten, frying pan, bird, pig's head, sewing needle, spoon, cane, and a crescent moon.

Headed West

The Clarks are heading west. Little do they know they are taking along some things they can't see. Find the wrench, ice-cream cone, fish, mushroom, wishbone, stool, screw, letter **W**, pencil, walnut, teacup, nail, and the envelope.

The Opera

It's the final scene of the opera. Hidden objects surround the players and the audience. See if you can find a fish, apron, rabbit's head, closed umbrella, flowerpot, teacup, apple, mouse, pail, safety pin, wrench, banana, carrot, tree, sailboat, snail, ice-cream cone, and a spoon.

The Busy Beaver

Beaver is so busy bringing more wood for his dam that he doesn't notice fourteen hidden objects. Can you find a deer, heart, saw, banana, bell, bird, hat, duck, artist's paintbrush, horn, comb, eagle's head, ring, and a fork?

Something to Crow About

Jeff's scarecrow can't scare away the crows or the hidden objects around the garden. Can you "weed out" a duck, glove, banana, trowel, mouse, scissors, butterfly, ice-cream pop, artist's paintbrush, and a carrot?

Fish Ride

Before Jeremy finishes his ride on the back of the fish, find a snake, witch's head, canoe, two fish, swan, turtle, dragonfly, sea horse, mouse, elf's head, and a man's profile.

Summer Theater

Tom and Leah entertain their friends with an original musical. As they sing, find a spoon, paper clip, teacup, mushroom, carrot, sewing needle, butterfly, harmonica, heart, clock, and a megaphone hidden on the stage.

Haunted House

Wendy Witch is leaving for her Halloween ride. Before she returns, see if you can locate the thirty-seven hidden objects around the haunted house: a flashlight, horseshoe, hammer, chess piece, butter knife, comb, open umbrella, feather duster, toothbrush, pencil, book, hairbrush, screwdriver, and twenty-four ghosts.

Woodland Harmony

Frog is delighted with the clever way the animals provide musical instruments for the symphony. Are you clever enough to find fourteen hidden objects? Spot the sailboat, rabbit, airplane, canoe, baseball bat, key, bird, muffin, horse's head, coffeepot, king's head, earphones, cat, and the loaf of bread.

Ice Hockey

Who will score a goal? Who will locate the hidden objects? Find a fishhook, arrow, plunger, cowboy hat, hairbrush, coffeepot, spoon, key, sewing needle, paper clip, heart, mallet, pencil, and a handbell.

Giddyup

Getting the horse to go is the hardest part of riding. It's also hard to find the fifteen hidden objects: a cat's head, spoon, necktie, muffin, fish, book, cane, hockey stick, toothbrush, pencil, football, vase, envelope, paper airplane, and a jump rope.

Family Camping

Everyone's busy having fun at the campsite, so they haven't noticed the twelve hidden objects. You can have fun finding a wishbone, artist's paintbrush, acorn, feather, key, bell, toothbrush, ice-cream pop, hatchet, radish, pencil, and a safety pin.

Christmas Caroling

Caroling is one of the traditions of the holiday season. While the carolers make joyous music, try to find a banana, bird, gift, Santa's head, pine tree, bell, skateboard, mug, nutcracker soldier, sleigh, clothespin, comb, ice skate, stocking, padlock, hammer, and a Christmas ornament.

Cowtown

Kent notices all the cows as his family reaches the outskirts of Cowtown. But he doesn't notice the nineteen hidden objects. Do you? Find a girl's head, seal, hammer, elephant's head, piece of pie, crayon, baseball cap, broom, artist's paintbrush, carrot, piece of cake, ice-cream scoop, apple, whistle, flashlight, boot, key, toothbrush, and a spatula.

Hidden Hounds

The horse and rider are so intent on their mission that they have no idea there are twenty hounds coming along with them. Can you find all twenty hidden hounds?

Grocery Shopping

On grocery-shopping day everyone has favorite foods to buy. Can you "shop" for the eleven hidden objects in the store? Look for a ladder, toothbrush, pocket watch, golf club, flyswatter, golf flag, shoe, trowel, teacup, sailboat, and a knitted hat.

Kids' Lost Clothes

Larry and Rosanne and their little dog are trying to imagine where all their missing items can be. Do you think they should look more closely around the room to find a dog's leash, two jackets, four boots, two knitted hats, two scarves, two mittens, and two gloves?

Penguin Suits

The Penguin brothers are excited about opening their new store. Around them are thirteen hidden objects: a turtle, paintbrush, key, knitted hat, book, vase, spoon, nail, paper clip, bell, pencil, mallet, and a floor lamp. Can you find them all?

Plymouth Harvest

Pilgrim children help bring in the harvest. Can you "harvest" all fourteen hidden objects from the field? Look for a comb, key, cat, candle, pliers, loaf of bread, paintbrush, bird, oar, pencil, purse, rabbit's head, exclamation point, and a pelican.

Rehearsal—A Moment of Chaos

All the students have a part to play in the spring festival. Your part is finding all twenty-eight hidden objects on the stage. See if you can spot a carrot, closed umbrella, broom, radish, spatula, iron, frying pan, paint roller, ladle, plunger, dinosaur, mallet, duck, hairbrush, feather, oilcan, fish,

golf club, piece of cake with a candle, dustpan, turkey drumstick, pig, bird, flag, baseball bat, saltshaker, mouse, and a rabbit.

Catnap

The cat doesn't know that the mice are playing all around him, and no one knows there are thirteen hidden objects in the room. You can outsmart all of them by finding a banana, fish, boot, mushroom, candle, toothbrush, bone, dog's head, sailboat, teacup, crescent moon, tongs, and a comb.

Babe Didrikson Zaharias

This famous golfer impressed many people in the course of her career. You can make a good impression, too, by finding a nail, baseball helmet, mug, fife, trowel, duck's head, banana, hammer, pig, snake, boot, slice of lemon, and a saltshaker hidden in the picture.

Tree House

This tree house makes a wonderful hideaway, and this picture makes a great place for thirteen hidden objects. Can you discover the fish, paper clip, ice-cream cone, baseball bat, rabbit, open book, candle, hammer, artist's paintbrush, cat, hockey stick, toothbrush, and the heart?

In the Clouds

Flying high in the clouds can be great fun, and it's also fun to locate all fourteen hidden objects in this picture. Can you find a whale, artist's paintbrush, rabbit, pliers, spoon, boot, envelope, ladder, carrot, toothbrush, magnifying glass, Santa's cap, penguin, and a camel?

Signing the Declaration

The signers of the Declaration of Independence were busy making history, never realizing that there were thirteen hidden objects in the room with them. Find a pennant, candle, sailboat, ice skate, artist's paintbrush, mouse, flashlight, flute, fish, hammer, ice-cream cone, nail, and a bird.

Monkey Fun

The monkeys' favorite pastime is thinking and talking about bananas. Maybe your favorite thing is finding hidden objects in this scene. Find a spoon, bird, pine tree, fork, horse's head, toucan, rabbit, deer, fish, pencil, and a paw print.

Holiday Wreath

There are twenty objects hiding in this wreath. How fast can you find a pear, heart, candle, teacup, pencil, magnet, bell, angel, apple, artist's paintbrush, bone, ice-cream pop, mushroom, piece of pie, necklace, spoon, acorn, three-leaf clover, butterfly, and a nail?

Fun by the Stream

The kids are so interested in what they have in the pail that they don't see what's hiding around them. Find a stalk of celery, bell, button, feather, envelope, elephant's head, pencil, key, baseball cap, spoon, hairbrush, scissors, and a chicken.

Playful Otters

The otters are having fun at the waterfall. While they frolic, see how fast you can find a rabbit, snake, arrowhead, spoon, teacup, lizard, rooster, and two birds.

Safari Treasure

The journey ends in success when Rich and Spot discover the hidden treasure. Now find the other hidden treasure: a sailboat, duck, number 9, spoon, number 5, slice of pizza, cat, flowerpot, camel, chicken, fox, telescope, artist's paintbrush, safety pin, candle, and a tack.

Kittens at Play

Three of the kittens get into mischief while the other one sleeps. You won't be caught napping if you can find a bird, heart, slice of cheese, crescent moon, candle, feather, nail, muffin, ice-cream cone, flashlight, whistle, and a seashell hidden in the picture.

Forest Friends

The doe is alert for sounds and smells while her fawn eats. Are you alert, too? Find out by spotting the hidden objects around them: a broom, clarinet, paintbrush, baseball bat, raccoon, squirrel, sailboat, banana, turtle's head, hairbrush, tepee, spoon, bird, lollipop, and a rag doll.

Camping Out

Brad and Wayne are having a great time camping out and listening to the crickets. You can't hear them, but can you find twelve crickets hidden around the campsite?

Salamanders' Tea Party

The salamanders are enjoying a creative tea party. You can join in the fun by finding a rabbit, party hat, purse, chick, hockey stick, knitted hat, crescent moon, ring, heart, shoe, bird, cupcake, and a magnet.

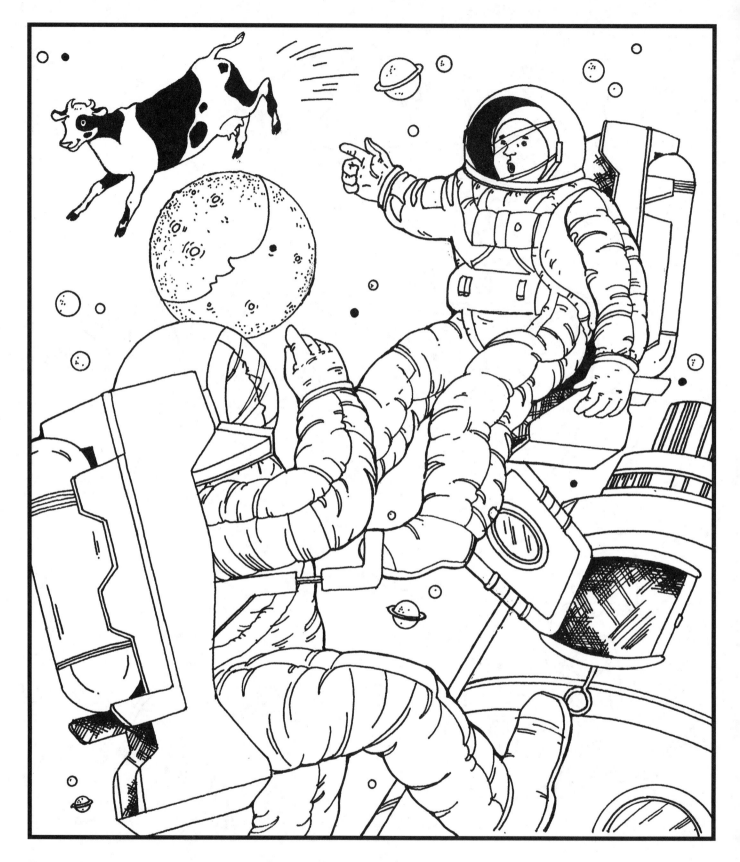

Space Walk

The astronauts are so astonished by the cow jumping over the moon that they don't notice the thirteen hidden objects out in space. Can you find a sailboat, golf club, bird, coat hanger, wrench, toothbrush, fish, piece of pie, mallet, mushroom, horse, dinosaur, and a ring?

Easter Rabbits

The Easter rabbits are ready for the egg hunt to begin. You can start your own hunt by looking for the hidden objects around them: a butter knife, bat, goose, artist's paintbrush, caterpillar, pig's head, book, frog, feather, shovel, sailboat, and a bird.

Christmas Story

The children delight in Grandmother's reading of a Christmas fantasy. Use your imagination to find the twenty objects hidden around the room: a fishhook, pencil, roller skate, adhesive bandage, bird's head, egg, arrow, clothespin, spoon, heart, ladder, bell, toothbrush, string of sausage, slice of watermelon, magnet, light bulb, ice-cream cone, sewing needle, and a ring.

Rabbits Go to Market

Mother Rabbit takes Randy Rabbit to the market so they can fill their empty baskets. Fill your basket with the hidden objects in this picture: a teapot, bell, duck, fish, artist's paintbrush, toothbrush, ring, man's head, broom, ax, rolling pin, screwdriver, ice-cream cone, spoon, snake, pig's head, and a kite.

Pilgrim Harvest

Every Pilgrim has a task to perform during harvest season. Your task is to find the hidden objects: a comb, candle, mouse, rabbit, flower, slice of pizza, crochet hook, glove, paintbrush, mug, pushpin, and a slice of bread.

Elephant's Shower

A spring shower is a refreshing treat. While the elephant sprays himself, find a glove, shoe, spoon, pair of pants, horn, boomerang, football, egg, bird, shark, crown, eagle's head, and a heart hidden around this scene.

Blast-off!

The technicians at Mission Control monitor the blast-off. While they track the location of the rocket, can you spot these hidden objects: a dog's head, pig, pencil, spoon, sewing needle, bat, teacup, dolphin,

artist's paintbrush, saw, toothbrush, fish, duck, wristwatch, baseball, bird, ball-point pen, sailboat, baseball bat, flower, apple, comb, cat, rooster, dog, and a football?

Slumber Party

The mice welcome the cat to their slumber party. Before the cat gets any ideas, see if you can find a dog's head, carrot, sliced loaf of bread, pencil, mug, shovel, seal, lollipop, piece of cake, piece of pie, pushpin, and a sailboat hidden in and around the mouse house.

Roll to the Finish Line

Antonio and Sean race to the finish line. Before they get there, see if you can find thirteen hidden objects in this picture: a snake, ice-cream cone, spoon, milk carton, iron, comb, toothbrush, fish, teacup, egg, adhesive bandage, pencil, and a bear's head.

Team Photo

The team mascot interrupts the photo session with a friendly leap. Don't let anything interrupt you until you find a hidden dragonfly, fish, artist's paintbrush, ladle, piece of pie, exclamation point, telephone receiver, comb, bird, ice skate, feather, turkey drumstick, ring, and teacup.

Mr. Magico

Mr. Magico can pull a rabbit out of a hat, but can you spot twelve hidden objects in this picture? Find a piece of cake, trowel, toothbrush, baseball cap, piece of pie, artist's paintbrush, handbell, banana, lamp, teakettle, ladle, and a mug.

Sailing Ships

The kids' two wooden boats sail down the stream. There are eleven more boats hidden in this picture. Can you find all of them?

Wee Willie Winkie

Wee Willie is hurrying so fast through the streets that he fails to notice the hidden objects around him. See how fast you can find a pot, coat hanger, acorn, hammer, clothespin, teakettle, bowling pin, sock, telescope, heart, and a Viking ship.

Leopard's Flight

The monkeys are amazed to see the leopard flying overhead. As he approaches land, see if you can find a screw, spoon, stork, heart, handbell, comb, octopus, hat, bow, in-line skate, ice-cream cone, and a fishhook hidden in the picture.

Bird Watchers

While the bird watchers are on the lookout for an unusual kind of bird, try to spot the thirteen objects hidden in this picture: a cat, ladle, hamburger, turtle, bear, knitted hat, sailboat, carrot, apple, seal, wrench, toothbrush, and a wishbone.

Curious Bear Cubs

If the bear cubs get too close, the skunks will offer a smelly greeting. Before they do, find a fox's head, trowel, ice-cream cone, canoe, boot, fish, sock, carrot, dinosaur, pear, turtle, scissors, and a candle hidden around the animals.

Underwater Diver

The diver is ready to bring up his treasure. You can have your own treasure hunt as you look for the hidden objects: a baby's rattle, magnifying glass, light bulb, artist's paintbrush, safety pin, carrot, bunch of grapes, bell, wedge of cheese, key, pencil, and a slice of pizza.

Crossing the Plains

The Native Americans are moving their village. The children play a game as they go, and you can, too, by finding sixteen objects hidden around them: a buffalo, fish, bird, top, pencil, screw, bunch of grapes, snake, feather, moccasin, drum, fork, lizard, iron, paper clip, and a tepee.

Frog Went A-Courting

Frog is confident he can win his lady with a bouquet of flowers and kind words. You can be confident of finding all twelve hidden objects on the road to That Way: a rabbit, pig, pumpkin, teapot, sailboat, king, telescope, seal, shoe, fish, bell, and a bird.

Merry Musical Elves

While the elves make merry, find a parachute, doll, cane, teddy bear, cutting board, apron, kite, bell, baseball bat, hat, closed umbrella, scrub brush, toothbrush, hoe, rowboat, and an elf's shoe.

Unicorn Country

The unicorns and the princess are about to cross the moat into the castle. Before they reach home, see if you can find a fish, bird, swan, hamster, sewing needle, feather, heart, screw, nail, pliers, and a witch's hat.

Pizza Time

The bears can't wait to dig into their delicious pizza. Find sixteen hidden objects—a spoon, ruler, shoe, squirrel, hairbrush, nail, bird, bell, mouse, mug, fork, pencil, frying pan, sock, penguin, and a frog—before they finish their meal.

Hiking Across the Stream

Tina must pay attention when she crosses the stream. Maybe she will find the eighteen hidden objects along the way. Will she spot a deer's head, frog, rabbit, penguin, turtle, crane, snake, fox, zebra's head, ant, seal, mouse, butterfly, bird, leopard's head, fish, bee, and a ladybug?

Mouse in the House

Margie Mouse takes a shortcut through the living room and causes quite a stir. See if you can discover a shortcut to finding the fourteen hidden objects in the room: a pot, piece of pie, ear of corn, flashlight, butterfly, dog's head, fish, candle, spoon, ice-cream cone, turtle, wishbone, megaphone, and a cupcake.

The Bell Ringer

Jack rings the bell with such vigor that all ears have to be covered. Perhaps you can find fourteen objects hidden in this scene: a cat, airplane, telephone receiver, clothespin, apple, sailboat, ice-cream cone, kite, poodle's head, mushroom, owl, spoon, porcupine, and a banana.

Rip Van Winkle

Rip Van Winkle had a long nap. It won't take you twenty years to find the hidden objects in this picture: a butterfly, toothbrush, flashlight, ice-cream cone, piece of cake, paintbrush, teapot, book, light bulb, wrench, and a flower.

72

Raggedy Ann Doll

Teresa tells Raggedy Ann her secrets, but neither of them knows there are a dozen objects secretly hidden all around them. See if you can discover a fish, dog, rabbit, turtle, toy car, wooden deer, snake, squirrel, alligator, frog, pig, and a bird.

Snorkeling

Discovering underwater surprises is an exciting adventure. See if you can find the fourteen "surprises" hidden in this picture: a bow, ice-cream cone, rabbit's head, high-heeled shoe, carrot, pitchfork, barbell, banana, snail, apple, tack, penguin, tweezers, and a question mark.

The Mayflower at Anchor

The Pilgrims have brought along fourteen objects hidden on and around the Mayflower. Can you find a butterfly, frying pan, open umbrella, closed umbrella, iron, boot, carrot, ladder, pencil, artist's paintbrush, piece of pie, swan's head, stocking, and a pair of pants?

On the Farm

Completing all the farm chores sometimes takes a long time. But it shouldn't take you very long to find sixteen objects hidden in the farmyard: a pot, football, ice-cream cone, magnet, picture frame, sickle, glove, crayon, spool of thread, hot dog, comb, heart, ladder, open book, fish, and a pitchfork.

Davy Crockett and the Mountain Lion

Davy Crockett's attention is focused on the mountain lion. Focusing your attention on the hidden objects will reveal them in no time. Can you see a clam, squirrel, shark, rabbit, mushroom, lollipop, toothbrush, shoe, flamingo's head, and a fish hidden in this picture?

Dog Takes a Bath

After Frisky gets his bath, it will be Goldy's turn. As they dry off, find seventeen objects hidden in this backyard scene: a mouse, crane, alligator, shark, horse, ice-cream cone, cat, toy car, sewing needle, clothespin, butterfly, sock, hat, bird, sailboat, boot, and a saltshaker.

Paddlefish

The paddlefish sees many fish underwater, but he doesn't see any of the thirteen objects hidden around him. Do you see a balloon, mouse, sock, artist's paintbrush, toothbrush, heart, slice of bread, hat, slipper, chipmunk, bird, bow, and a high-heeled shoe?

Ghostly Mail

Georgie Ghost has received a letter from his cousin Gertrude telling him there are twenty-one objects hidden around his house. Can you find all of them? There's a bird, seal, turnip, turtle, spoon, screwdriver, bat, ladder, open book, pencil, top hat, flamingo, pickax, cat's head, giraffe, fish, owl, the letters **V** and **H**, and two cherries.

Building a Robot

Professor Pendergast had to be very clever to build Ronald Robot. You have to be clever to find all sixteen hidden objects in his basement: a comb, nail, artist's paintbrush, book, pennant, hoe, toy truck, piece of cake, toothbrush, three-leaf clover, key, banana, saltshaker, cup, pliers, and a safety pin.

Stickball in the City

Mother wants the children to scoot, but almost everyone else in the neighborhood is enjoying the game of stickball. Enjoy finding a ladle, boomerang, paintbrush, telephone receiver, sailboat, boot, mitten, ice-cream cone, bow, hammer, piece of pie, hockey stick, and an open book hidden in this picture.

Hide-and-Seek

It's fun to play hide-and-seek with your friends, and it's also fun to seek the twelve objects hiding in this backyard scene: a ladder, book, nail, trowel, paintbrush, ring, mitten, toothbrush, tire pump, key, golf club, and a paper clip.

Journey to Outer Space

The astronauts see many unusual objects while exploring outer space. But there are even more objects hidden from their view: a ring, telescope, slipper, spool of thread, wrench, scissors, ice-cream pop, television set, bell, teacup, envelope, light bulb, and two toothbrushes.

Icarus

Before Icarus flies too close to the sun, see if you can spot the hidden objects: a mouse, padlock, teacup, spoon, seal, candle, dog's head, slipper, dinosaur's head, heart, and two birds.

It's Only a Mouse

When the elephant sees the tiny mouse, there is big trouble in the rain forest. Finding all thirty-one objects hidden in this scene is a big challenge. Good luck in finding a trowel, sailboat, rabbit, pine tree, bull's head, fork, hammer, teapot, lizard, shark, slipper, comb, horse's head, telephone receiver, fish,

candle, carrot, sock, can, tooth, toucan's head, fox's head, teacup, needle and thread, paper bag, ring, toothbrush, snail, spoon, pencil, and a button.

Archaeology

Archaeological digs can reveal some interesting artifacts. See if you can reveal the undiscovered objects in this picture: a coffeepot, funnel, toothbrush, ice-cream cone, scrub brush, iron, jar, cup and saucer, piece of cake, teapot, bell, and a flashlight.

Stampede!

The cowboys struggle to control the stampeding cattle. With a lot less effort you'll be able to find a hat, puzzle piece, mug, bat, comb, campfire, boot, tied bandanna, bird, and a sheriff's badge hidden in this picture.

Snails

The snails are exploring beneath the mushrooms. We don't know what they might find, but you can find twelve hidden objects: a barbell, trowel, bowling pin, hat, sailing ship, hatchet, fish, toy car, sea gull, sailboat, lemon, and a bird.

Sonja Henie

Becoming a famous figure skater takes many years of practice. It won't take you long, though, to discover the hidden objects on the ice rink: a coin, hat, snail, ear of corn, pliers, fish, snake, boot, eagle's head, dove, telescope, handbell, mushroom, heart, toothbrush, cap, and a glass.

Sunken Treasure

Hidden in and around the shipwreck are twelve objects. Dive down and find a fishing pole, recorder, bottle, telephone receiver, knitted hat, light bulb, teacup, snail, ladder, toothbrush, tomato, and a butter knife.

The Excursion Train

Everyone scurries to the train so they won't miss out on the fun. You can get in on the fun, too, by looking for the objects hidden on and around the train: a stalk of broccoli, wedding ring, apple, tape measure, hairbrush, stocking, rabbit's head, bird, feather, banjo, toothbrush, boot, fish, vulture, and a ladder.

Mowing the Lawn

Mowing the lawn can be a pleasant chore when friends pass by. Before Raccoon finishes his task, see if you can find fourteen objects hidden in the picture: a pencil, closed umbrella, metal nut, bowl, nail, squirrel, lizard, iron, mouse, frog, hammer, fork, teacup, and a penguin.

"thistle"

cirsium undulatum

Salamander School

The lesson for today in Salamander School is about flowers. Your assignment is to find all sixteen objects hidden in this outdoor classroom: a fish, shoe, duck, closed umbrella, butterfly, boot, envelope, rabbit, car, bird, dog, fox, ladle, pig, carrot, and a turtle.

Ride 'em Cowboy

It takes some imagination to think you're "riding the range" in front of the barbershop. Use your imagination to find the objects hidden in this picture: a carrot, wristwatch, artist's paintbrush, toothbrush, pear, sock, telephone receiver, flashlight, key, mallet, pencil, comb, and a cap.

96

Elf and Mouse

The elf and mouse are having a galloping good time. You can have a good time discovering the hidden objects they haven't even noticed: a rabbit, iron, sewing needle, toothbrush, fish, pear, ice-cream cone, telescope, button, scissors, duck, and a cane.

Volleyball Game

Volleyball is a game of skill and fun. You can exercise your skill by finding a hairbrush, comb, pencil, mug, spool of thread, pillow, pinwheel, banana, baseball cap, loaf of bread, ruler, clothespin, bottle, fish, bird, and two soda cans hidden in the gymnasium.

Alice in Wonderland

Alice tells the Cheshire Cat about her adventures in Wonderland. Before the cat fades away, see if you can find all the hidden objects in this picture: a key, book, teapot, jar, piece of cake, rabbit, teacup, top hat, apple core, mouse, pocket watch, and a crown.

Raking the Garden

The rabbits are tidying up the fall leaves. See how many hidden objects you can "rake in": a jump rope, mouse, butterfly, baseball, comb, slipper, dolphin, fish, sailboat, ruler, flashlight, pear, and a duck.

Turtles Take a Break

The turtles are enjoying a sunny afternoon. Can you find a pot, feather, piece of pie, saw, butterfly, owl, wishbone, snake, pickax, carrot, bird, canoe, and a pencil hidden among the lily pads?

Pet Store

The pet store owner will give Tim twelve hidden objects from his store in exchange for the cat. Can you help Tim make the trade by finding a duck, golf club, flashlight, piece of cake, hat, screwdriver, seal, sock, spoon, slipper, rolling pin, and a nail?

102

Hovering Hummingbirds

The hummingbirds hover around the flowers searching for nectar. Can you hover over this picture until you find thirteen hidden objects? Look for a hat, pen in inkwell, horn, key, swan, hourglass, ladle, owl, eyeglasses, trowel, starfish, slice of watermelon, and a teacup.

Charles Lindbergh

When Lindbergh landed "The Spirit of St. Louis" in Paris, there was great jubilation. In the midst of the celebration can you spot a pot, sewing needle, ring, safety pin, balloon, whale, shoe, nail, goose, teacup, mushroom, slice of lemon, and a butter knife hidden in the picture?

Mouse and Grasshopper

The mouse and the grasshopper have brought more to the picnic than what's in the basket. Can you find a baseball bat, dinosaur, ice-cream cone, life preserver, dog's head, shark, book, olive, banana, fish, boy's head, rabbit's head, nutcracker, light bulb, and two birds hidden in the picture?

Beach Turtles

While the young turtles build their sand castle, see if you can find a teakettle, paper clip, iron, boot, party hat, sock, toothbrush, pear, pencil, fishhook, spoon, ice-cream cone, plunger, and a nail hidden on the beach.

On Frozen Pond

The frozen pond is a great place to play and a great place to hide objects. Can you find a frying pan, loaf of bread, worm, bow, spool of thread, bird, ice-cream cone, padlock, paper cup, sock, piece of pie, ax, handbell, and a peanut?

Hungry Chipmunks

While the chipmunks hunt for food, see if you can find the objects hidden in the tree: a butterfly, mitten, feather, shark, bird, mallet, hummingbird, magnet, cat, starfish, and an arrowhead.

Rabbit Picnic

The Bunny family's picnic basket is empty. Can you help them find the fifteen missing carrots so they can have lunch?

Dinosaurs

Dinosaurs are extinct. The thirty hidden objects in this giant scene are not. Can you find a rake, loaf of bread, owl, horse's head, rabbit, ant, penguin, piece of pie, hammer, rooster, spoon, witch's head,

seashell, sailboat, fish, mouse, raccoon, lizard, fork, candle, knight's helmet, bird, gorilla's head, hat, snake, walrus's head, lion's head, seal, dog's head, and an eagle?

Making Valentines

While Lori makes a special valentine, can you find a fork, artist's paintbrush, whale, mallet, ruler, mouse, banana, penguin, pencil, apple, cowboy boot, toothbrush, and a coin among the ribbons and lace?

Digging in the Garden

While harvesting her garden crop, Joan discovers nineteen objects hidden among the vegetables. Can you find a snail, bug, shark, slice of bread, peeled banana, fish, seashell, cat's head, rabbit's head, turtle, tube of paint, ice-cream cone, crab, mushroom, whale, candle, screwdriver, bee, and a spoon?

Moon Walk

The mischievous Martian has fooled the space explorers. Before they discover what made the huge footprints, can you find these hidden objects: a book, jar, baseball cap, teacup, mitten, paintbrush, magnifying glass, toothbrush, piece of pie, bell, slipper, and a pencil?

Lemonade for Sale

There are fifteen objects hidden around the lemonade stand. Can you find a bell, fish, telephone receiver, whale, vase, dwarf's head, paintbrush, banana, adhesive bandage, megaphone, golf club, slice of bread, comb, book, and a teacup?

Toucan's Home

Can you find the hidden objects in the tropical home of the toucan? There's a dog's head, chicken, mouse, alligator's head, feather, toothbrush, mushroom, dog, bird, pear, slipper, and two fish.

President James Monroe

President Monroe took a three-month tour of the nation following his inauguration. See if you can find a pitcher, mouse, turkey, fish, carrot, loaf of bread, mitten, shoe, feather, cat, ice skate, rabbit's head, and a belt hidden in this rural scene.

Ghostly Chores

After Garry Ghost finishes mowing his lawn, his next chore is to find a seal, hat, shoe, piece of pie, sewing needle, screwdriver, book, lollipop, ladder, baseball bat, ice-cream cone, lamp, lamb, pennant, exclamation point, the letters **B** and **E**, and the number 4 hidden in the ghostly neighborhood.

Let's Celebrate!

Before the celebration begins, see if you can find a duck, butter knife, fish, piece of pie, mouse, purse, book, hat, sewing needle, light bulb, pencil, pear, artist's paintbrush, bird, rabbit, and two cherries hidden around the room.

Exploring the Northwest

When Sacagawea led the Lewis and Clark expedition down the river, she didn't know what they would find. There are twelve hidden objects for you to find: a fish, buffalo, butterfly, sheep, deer, mouse, rabbit, turtle, eagle, goose, bird, and a squirrel.

120

Baby Dino's Lunch

The baby dinosaur is so interested in his lunch that he hasn't noticed the fifteen hidden objects around him. Can you find a rabbit, ice-cream cone, turtle, sailboat, scissors, baseball cap, fish, duck, snake, dog's head, comb, caterpillar, teacup, football, and a bell?

Young Florence Nightingale

The dog likes playing hospital, but the cat wants to escape. Find a baseball cap, open book, saltshaker, egg, hammer, pumpkin, mask, pear, carrot, fish, canoe, ladle, and a boot hidden in the picture.

Space Patrol

Amazing things happen while on space patrol. Among the strange sights are thirteen hidden objects. Can you find a coffeepot, nail, open umbrella, ladle, shoe, hat, crayon, orange, ring, baseball, canoe, kite, and a golf club?

Butterfly Ballet

There are twelve objects hidden among the dancing butterflies. Can you find a hot-air balloon, birdhouse, plunger, pinwheel, pocket watch, boy's head, handbell, dog, peach, carrot, scissors, and a tepee?

Baking Day

Besides the treats on the windowsill and the ones coming out of the oven, there are fourteen hidden "treats." Can you find a boy's face, baseball, ice-cream cone, sock, pear, glove, fish, mouse, turtle, snake, hat, bird, eyeglasses, and a bell in the kitchen?

Australian Bus Ride

The animals' trip is over, but your job of finding all thirteen hidden objects in this picture is just beginning. Can you find a fan, mitten, fork, parrot, spoon, pencil, apple, nail, two socks, and three mice?

Fall Fun

Playing in the leaves is more fun than raking them. It's even more fun to find all the hidden objects in this scene. Look for a cow, fish, dinosaur, funnel, golf club, duck, cat, spoon, hammer, saltshaker, frog, carrot, chick, and a clothespin.

Little Bo Peep

Little Bo Peep has lost her lambs, and all thirteen are hiding in this picture. Can you help her find them so they can all go home?

Fun in the Topiary Garden

The children are having a great time playing in this topiary garden. Can you discover the hiding places of a crayon, sheep's head, book, mouse's head, pitcher, duck, flute, cat, steer's head, seahorse, wishbone, apple core, fox, turtle, and a teacup?

Mushroom Shelter

While the bunnies take cover under the mushroom, see if you can find all the objects hidden in this rainstorm: a scarf, snake, fish, heart, button, mouse, spoon, balloon, bird, sewing needle, and two artist's paintbrushes.

Quilting Bees

You will be as busy as these quilting bees until you find all fourteen objects hidden on and around the quilt. How fast can you find a pencil, scissors, rabbit's head, baseball cap, closed umbrella, slice of pizza, frying pan, safety pin, shark, sewing needle, banana, snail, the number 4, and a candle?

Pilgrims Reach Land

The Pilgrims have arrived in the New World, and there's more there than meets the eye. Find fourteen objects hidden in this scene: a bear, bird, golf club, rabbit, piece of pie, shovel, screwdriver, pliers, alligator, sewing needle, artist's paintbrush, key, boot, and a pitcher.

Wood Ducks Seek Shelter

The wood duck family is nestled among the reeds. Also nestled in this picture are thirteen hidden objects. Can you find a shark, rabbit, fish, lizard, mouse, pencil, butterfly, seahorse, spoon, seal, snake, bird, and a bat?

Robin Hood

What's hiding in Sherwood Forest? Look for a teapot, horn, flashlight, kite, banana, fish, bird, pencil, toothbrush, spoon, ring, teacup, turtle, cat, king's head, scissors, and a duck.

Thrushes at Rest

Concealed around the thrushes are eighteen objects. Can you find a duck, boot, mitten, pliers, sock, artist's paintbrush, cat, mouse, spoon, ear of corn, fishhook, flying insect, ladle, heart, sewing needle, star, and two fish?

The Witch's Cats

The old witch wants to take all her cats for a walk. Can you find all nineteen of them hidden in this picture?

The House Painter

The painter has applied a fresh coat of paint, but there are still eleven objects hidden in this picture. Can you find a hamburger, shovel, scissors, teacup, ring, lollipop, saltshaker, fountain pen, skateboard, acorn, and a crayon?

137

The Birthday Cake

While the elves are putting the finishing touches on the birthday cake, see if you can find a balloon, glove, present, ice-cream cone, safety pin, rabbit, wrapped piece of candy, dog's head, spoon, duck, eyeglasses, paper cup, banana, sock, and a potato hidden in the bakery.

Napping Together

The cat is amazed to see a mouse napping with his friend. He'd be more amazed if he knew there are seventeen objects hidden in the room: a pennant, purse, fishing pole, acorn, artist's paintbrush, dragonfly, toothbrush, sailboat, rooster, butterfly, fish, hat, trowel, heart, bird, crescent moon, and a mushroom.

Cowboy in the Saddle

While the cowboy enjoys riding the range, see if you can discover a mouse, alligator, canoe, snake, bonnet, cat, chicken, teacup, boomerang, dog's head, bowl, cane, spatula, and a shoe concealed around the desert landscape.

Secret Recipes

The kittens aren't the only ones with a secret. There are fourteen objects secretly hidden in this scene: a crayon, fish, muffin, oar, ice-cream pop, sailboat, kite, rabbit, key, banana, artist's paintbrush, slipper, trowel, and a duck.

Three Bears and the B's

All fifteen hidden objects around Goldilocks and the bears begin with the letter B. Can you find a balloon, book, bell, bread, barn, bee, bunny, butterfly, bird, bat, banana, brush, baseball, boat, and a baseball bat before Goldilocks runs away?

142

Tag Football

Playing tag football is fun for everyone. So is finding hidden objects. In this outdoor scene see if you can spot a cat, piece of pie, horse, open umbrella, carrot, mallet, mouse, bird, snake, comb, spoon, saltshaker, wishbone, snail, artist's paintbrush, and a chicken.

Decorating the Tree

What fun to spend time together putting ornaments on the tree. There are thirteen hidden "ornaments" around the room: a magnet, sock, eyeglasses, whale, comb, in-line skate, book, button, bell, star, mitten, knitted hat, and a shoe.

144

A Day on the Farm

Seth is so excited about his visit to Uncle Jim's farm that he doesn't notice fourteen hidden objects. Do you see a whale, rabbit, ruler, open book, mug, platter, dog's head, spatula, lizard, spoon, fish, artist's paintbrush, gorilla's head, and a pencil?

Pigs in Love

Portia and Patrick Pig are so in love that they don't notice the sixteen objects hidden around them. Can you find a mouse, open umbrella, eyeglasses, gingerbread boy, baseball bat, thong sandal, hat, teacup, cupcake, spoon, pencil, saltshaker, chef's head, mallet, sock, and a cat's head?

Summertime at the North Pole

Playing checkers helps the elves keep busy. You can keep busy, too, by looking for the hidden objects in the room. Can you find a screwdriver, envelope, coin, sock, padlock, mallet, eyeglasses, butterfly, slice of bread, book, ice-cream cone, and a nail?

Gathering Mushrooms

While Jessica gathers mushrooms, see if you can gather the hidden objects in this picture. Find a dolphin, ice-cream cone, boot, hummingbird, bird, light bulb, open umbrella, strawberry, pear, hat, goose, lemon wedge, pine tree, deer's head, seal's head, bell, and a mouse.

Bunnies in Bunks

All the bunnies are tucked into their bunks for the night. Also tucked into this bunny bedroom are twenty hidden objects: a lima bean, ax, ice-cream cone, kite, arrow, toothbrush, tack, flowerpot, ladle, piece of cake, pencil, spool of thread, sailboat, hoe, crown, sewing needle, heart, artist's paintbrush, recorder, and a bell.

Honey Tree

Bear is sorry he tried to steal the bees' honey! Looking for the hidden objects around him is much safer. Can you find a comb, spoon, artist's paintbrush, fox's head, ice-cream cone, squirrel, hawk, teacup, glove, banana, eyeglasses, and a chicken's head?

150

Author at Work

When Marjorie Kinnan Rawlings wrote **The Yearling,** she visualized scenes for her book. Hidden in her thoughts and in the room are seventeen hidden objects: a horse, mushroom, toothbrush, whale, pea pod, hat, boot, cat, bone, lemon wedge, duck, flashlight, thimble, fork, nutcracker, ceramic jar, and a candle.

Sherlock Holmes

The master detective is looking for clues and doesn't realize there are fourteen objects hidden all around him. Can you find a banana, pair of dice, belt, rabbit, padlock, seal, baseball, pencil, heart, crayon, turtle, apple, and two doughnuts?

The Bow Wows in Concert

While the Bow Wows belt out their latest hit, see if you can find thirteen objects hidden around them. Look for a key, coat hanger, pear, golf club, tack, mug, fish, ice pop, ring, carrot, broom, pencil, and a book.

153

Flowers for Mom

Rachel and Roland Rabbit have surprised their mother with spring bouquets. They'd all be surprised to know that there are fourteen objects hidden nearby. Can you find a wristwatch, spoon, screwdriver, cap, jump rope, comb, cowboy hat, coin, hummingbird, pencil, T-shirt, pinwheel, tent, and a rake?

Nap Time

While Mom Dragon and her baby enjoy their afternoon nap, quietly search for a bell, closed umbrella, dog's head, vase, fish, musical note, tweezers, bird, rabbit's head, spoon, bone, mitten, three-leaf clover, butterfly, snake, swan, cat, key, and a beet.

Sea Turtle

The sea turtle doesn't know that there are sixteen objects swimming with him. Can you find them? Look for a goose, lizard, spoon, dress, eyeglasses, open book, eagle's head, high-heeled shoe, clown's head, toucan, penguin, snail, banana, dog, heart, and a ring.

Goldilocks

While Goldilocks gobbles the porridge, see if you can find a saw, spider, goose, antelope, pea pod, sheep, carrot, egg, beaver, ladybug, rabbit, mouse, elephant, and a banana before the bears get home.

Afternoon in the Garden

While Monique and her mother enjoy some quiet time together, see if you can find seventeen objects hidden in this scene. Look for a spatula, crab, acorn, arrow, spool of thread, cap, sailboat, letter **A**, shoe, clam shell, parrot, pliers, cat, bird, piece of pie, ice-cream cone, and a tube of toothpaste.

Daisy Stops the Train

Daring Daisy has decided to rest on the tracks! While Barney Beaver tries to get her to move, see if you can find a mitten, spoon, key, mug, shoe, magnifying glass, book, acorn, hairbrush, wrench, pencil, and a spatula.

Troubadors

Imagine hearing the lovely medieval music as you search for a bird, open book, swan, carrot, banana, bell, pear, horse, dragonfly, envelope, butterfly, crown, cake, fork, and a dog.

Hot Buttered Popcorn

Patrick is so hungry for the popcorn that he doesn't see the fourteen hidden objects. Find a turtle, derby hat, pencil, bonnet, ruler, acorn, envelope, clown's head, turkey, jump rope, adhesive bandage, elephant's head, wrapped piece of candy, and a bird.

Clover Tea, Please

Shirley Sheep sips steaming tea. Before she finishes, can you find a carrot, penguin, snail, hot-air balloon, open umbrella, sock, key on a key ring, accordion, pine tree, coat hanger, number 7, wishbone, feather, cotton candy, and a diamond ring?

Autumn Wind

While Jenny and Jared try to catch Jared's cap, see if you can locate the thirteen hidden objects that have "blown" into the scene. Find a nail, artist's paintbrush, fish, piece of cake, toothbrush, shoe, screwdriver, cupcake, mouse, chicken drumstick, peeled banana, pliers, and a hammer.

Tennis, Anyone?

Everyone's ready for Tracy's next serve. Are you ready to find twelve objects hidden in this scene? Look for a golf club, cat, trowel, letter **A**, hammer, ice-cream cone, banana, mug, sailboat, turtle, sock, and a toothbrush.

At the Movies

The kids are enjoying the movie so much that they don't see the seventeen objects hidden in the theater. Find a fish, dog's head, canoe, bird, crescent moon, coat hanger, artist's paintbrush, dragonfly, tweezers, sailboat, mouse, flower, tube of paint, hairbrush, bee, butterfly, and a comb.

After the Blizzard

There's so much snow everywhere that the children don't notice all the hidden objects. Can you find a rabbit, sock, fish, teacup, light bulb, artist's paintbrush, pillow, teddy bear, handbell, Santa's hat, hammer, spoon, carrot, shovel, and a toothbrush?

Busy Beavers

The beavers are so busy building that they don't see the objects "built" in to this scene. Find a book, camera, key, iron, sewing needle, apple core, saw, lizard, hairbrush, pennant, paper clip, tube of toothpaste, and two birds.

167

ANSWERS

Cover: sewing needle, frying pan, flashlight, shoe, ice-cream pop, rabbit, artist's paintbrush, lady's head, boot, pencil, crown, golf club, ice-cream cone, bird, whistle, mallet

3: fish, spoon, orange, potato, pencil, snake, turtle, spring, magnet, bird, butter knife, whale, fork, feather

4: pot, question mark, trowel, dragonfly, artist's paintbrush, pennant, banana, screwdriver, bell, nail, frog, fish, snail, duck, wrench, candle, crescent moon, shoe, bone, two butterflies

5: candy cane, mitten, stocking, butterfly, artist's paintbrush, bird, pliers, sailboat, fish, deer's head, teapot, slipper, mouse

6: pineapple, lady's head, paper clip, teacup, milk carton, calculator, toothbrush, spoon, scissors, pail, tape dispenser, bird, feather, butterfly, rabbit, ice-cream cone, rose, whisk broom

7: horn, pennant, tack, sailboat, empty spool of thread, pencil, hammer, ice-cream cone, spoon, hairbrush, ladder, candle, iron

8: pot, turtle, light bulb, snail, wristwatch, mop, ax, cat, mouse, jet plane, screwdriver, butterfly

9: fishing pole, dog, seal, peanut, gingerbread man, shovel, fish, ring, lamb's head, mouse, sailboat, snowman, sock, banana, dog's head, top hat, carrot

10: turtle, saltshaker, jump rope, artist's paintbrush, sailboat, toothbrush, hat, carrot, fish, butterfly, bird, hammer, lizard

11: kite, sock, mitten, frying pan, bird, pig's head, sewing needle, spoon, cane, crescent moon

12: wrench, ice-cream cone, fish, mushroom, wishbone, stool, screw, letter **W**, pencil, walnut, teacup, nail, envelope

13: fish, apron, rabbit's head, closed umbrella, flowerpot, teacup, apple, mouse, pail, safety pin, wrench, banana, carrot, tree, sailboat, snail, ice-cream cone, spoon

14: deer, heart, saw, banana, bell, bird, hat, duck, artist's paintbrush, horn, comb, eagle's head, ring, fork

15: duck, glove, banana, trowel, mouse, scissors, butterfly, ice-cream pop, artist's paintbrush, carrot

16: snake, witch's head, canoe, two fish, swan, turtle, dragonfly, sea horse, mouse, elf's head, man's profile

17: spoon, paper clip, teacup, mushroom, carrot, sewing needle, butterfly, harmonica, heart, clock, megaphone

18: flashlight, horseshoe, hammer, chess piece, butter knife, comb, open umbrella, feather duster, toothbrush, pencil, book, hairbrush, screwdriver, twenty-four ghosts

19: sailboat, rabbit, airplane, canoe, baseball bat, key, bird, muffin, horse's head, coffeepot, king's head, earphones, cat, loaf of bread

20: fishhook, arrow, plunger, cowboy hat, hairbrush, coffeepot, spoon, key, sewing needle, paper clip, heart, mallet, pencil, handbell

21: cat's head, spoon, necktie, muffin, fish, book, cane, hockey stick, toothbrush, pencil, football, vase, envelope, paper airplane, jump rope

22: wishbone, artist's paintbrush, acorn, feather, key, bell, toothbrush, ice-cream pop, hatchet, radish, pencil, safety pin

23: banana, bird, gift, Santa's head, pine tree, bell, skateboard, mug, nutcracker soldier, sleigh, clothespin, comb, ice skate, stocking, padlock, hammer, Christmas ornament

24: girl's head, seal, hammer, elephant's head, piece of pie, crayon, baseball cap, broom, artist's paintbrush, carrot, piece of cake, ice-cream scoop, apple, whistle, flashlight, boot, key, toothbrush, spatula.

25: twenty hounds

26: ladder, toothbrush, pocket watch, golf club, flyswatter, golf flag, shoe, trowel, teacup, sailboat, knitted hat

27: dog's leash, two jackets, four boots, two knitted hats, two scarves, two mittens, two gloves

28: turtle, paintbrush, key, knitted hat, book, vase, spoon, nail, paper clip, bell, pencil, mallet, floor lamp

29: comb, key, cat, candle, pliers, loaf of bread, paintbrush, bird, oar, pencil, purse, rabbit's head, exclamation point, pelican

30-31: carrot, closed umbrella, broom, radish, spatula, iron, frying pan, paint roller, ladle, plunger, dinosaur, mallet, duck, hairbrush, feather, oilcan, fish, golf club, piece of cake with a candle, dustpan, turkey drumstick, pig, bird, flag, baseball bat, saltshaker, mouse, rabbit

32: banana, fish, boot, mushroom, candle, toothbrush, bone, dog's head, sailboat, teacup, crescent moon, tongs, comb

33: nail, baseball helmet, mug, fife, trowel, duck's head, banana, hammer, pig, snake, boot, slice of lemon, saltshaker

34: fish, paper clip, ice-cream cone, baseball bat, rabbit, open book, candle, hammer, artist's paintbrush, cat, hockey stick, toothbrush, heart

172

35: whale, artist's paintbrush, rabbit, pliers, spoon, boot, envelope, ladder, carrot, toothbrush, magnifying glass, Santa's cap, penguin, camel

36: pennant, candle, sailboat, ice skate, artist's paintbrush, mouse, flashlight, flute, fish, hammer, ice-cream cone, nail, bird

37: spoon, bird, pine tree, fork, horse's head, toucan, rabbit, deer, fish, pencil, and a paw print

38: pear, heart, candle, teacup, pencil, magnet, bell, angel, apple, artist's paintbrush, bone, ice-cream pop, mushroom, piece of pie, necklace, spoon, acorn, three-leaf clover, butterfly, nail

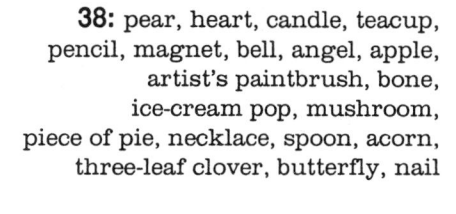

39: stalk of celery, bell, button, feather, envelope, elephant's head, pencil, key, baseball cap, spoon, hairbrush, scissors, chicken

40: rabbit, snake, arrowhead, spoon, teacup, lizard, rooster, two birds

41: sailboat, duck, number 9, spoon, number 5, slice of pizza, cat, flowerpot, camel, chicken, fox, telescope, artist's paintbrush, safety pin, candle, tack

173

42: bird, heart, slice of cheese, crescent moon, candle, feather, nail, muffin, ice-cream cone, flashlight, whistle, seashell

43: broom, clarinet, paintbrush, baseball bat, raccoon, squirrel, sailboat, banana, turtle's head, hairbrush, tepee, spoon, bird, lollipop, rag doll

44: twelve crickets

45: rabbit, party hat, purse, chick, hockey stick, knitted hat, crescent moon, ring, heart, shoe, bird, cupcake, magnet

46: sailboat, golf club, bird, coat hanger, wrench, toothbrush, fish, piece of pie, mallet, mushroom, horse, dinosaur, ring

47: butter knife, bat, goose, artist's paintbrush, caterpillar, pig's head, book, frog, feather, shovel, sailboat, bird

48: fishhook, pencil, roller skate, adhesive bandage, bird's head, egg, arrow, clothespin, spoon, heart, ladder, bell, toothbrush, string of sausage, slice of watermelon, magnet, light bulb, ice-cream cone, sewing needle, ring

49: teapot, bell, duck, fish, artist's paintbrush, toothbrush, ring, man's head, broom, ax, rolling pin, screwdriver, ice-cream cone, spoon, snake, pig's head, kite

50: comb, candle, mouse, rabbit, flower, slice of pizza, crochet hook, glove, paintbrush, mug, pushpin, slice of bread

51: glove, shoe, spoon, pair of pants, horn, boomerang, football, egg, bird, shark, crown, eagle's head, heart

52-53: dog's head, pig, pencil, spoon, sewing needle, bat, teacup, dolphin, artist's paintbrush, saw, toothbrush, fish, duck, wristwatch, baseball, bird, ball-point pen, sailboat, baseball bat, flower, apple, comb, cat, rooster, dog, football

54: dog's head, carrot, sliced loaf of bread, pencil, mug, shovel, seal, lollipop, piece of cake, piece of pie, pushpin, sailboat

55: snake, ice-cream cone, spoon, milk carton, iron, comb, toothbrush, fish, teacup, egg, adhesive bandage, pencil, bear's head

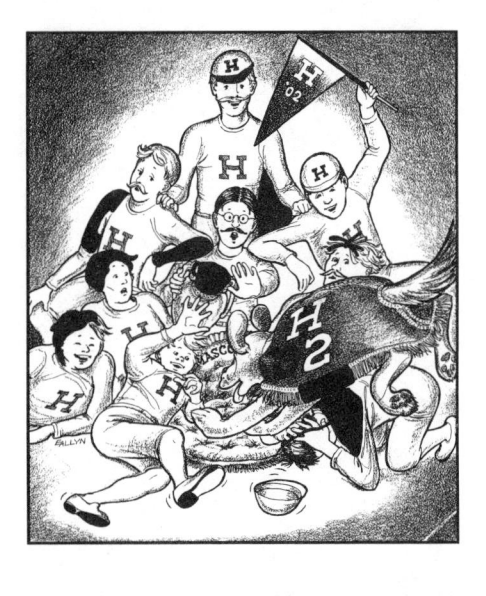

56: dragonfly, fish, artist's paintbrush, ladle, piece of pie, exclamation point, telephone receiver, comb, bird, ice skate, feather, turkey drumstick, ring, teacup

57: piece of cake, trowel, toothbrush, baseball cap, piece of pie, artist's paintbrush, handbell, banana, lamp, teakettle, ladle, mug

58: eleven boats

59: pot, coat hanger, acorn, hammer, clothespin, teakettle, bowling pin, sock, telescope, heart, Viking ship

60: screw, spoon, stork, heart, handbell, comb, octopus, hat, bow, in-line skate, ice-cream cone, fishhook

61: cat, ladle, hamburger, turtle, bear, knitted hat, sailboat, carrot, apple, seal, wrench, toothbrush, wishbone

62: fox's head, trowel, ice-cream cone, canoe, boot, fish, sock, carrot, dinosaur, pear, turtle, scissors, candle

63: baby's rattle, magnifying glass, light bulb, artist's paintbrush, safety pin, carrot, bunch of grapes, bell, wedge of cheese, key, pencil, slice of pizza

64: buffalo, fish, bird, top, pencil, screw, bunch of grapes, snake, feather, moccasin, drum, fork, lizard, iron, paper clip, tepee

65: rabbit, pig, pumpkin, teapot, sailboat, king, telescope, seal, shoe, fish, bell, bird

66: parachute, doll, cane, teddy bear, cutting board, apron, kite, bell, baseball bat, hat, closed umbrella, scrub brush, toothbrush, hoe, rowboat, elf's shoe

67: fish, bird, swan, hamster, sewing needle, feather, heart, screw, nail, pliers, witch's hat

68: spoon, ruler, shoe, squirrel, hairbrush, nail, bird, bell, mouse, mug, fork, pencil, frying pan, sock, penguin, frog

69: deer's head, frog, rabbit, penguin, turtle, crane, snake, fox, zebra's head, ant, seal, mouse, butterfly, bird, leopard's head, fish, bee, ladybug

70: pot, piece of pie, ear of corn, flashlight, butterfly, dog's head, fish, candle, spoon, ice-cream cone, turtle, wishbone, megaphone, cupcake

71: cat, airplane, telephone receiver, clothespin, apple, sailboat, ice-cream cone, kite, poodle's head, mushroom, owl, spoon, porcupine, banana

72: butterfly, toothbrush, flashlight, ice-cream cone, piece of cake, paintbrush, teapot, book, light bulb, wrench, flower

73: fish, dog, rabbit, turtle, toy car, wooden deer, snake, squirrel, alligator, frog, pig, bird

74: bow, ice-cream cone, rabbit's head, high-heeled shoe, carrot, pitchfork, barbell, banana, snail, apple, tack, penguin, tweezers, question mark

75: butterfly, frying pan, open umbrella, closed umbrella, iron, boot, carrot, ladder, pencil, artist's paintbrush, piece of pie, swan's head, stocking, pair of pants

76: pot, football, ice-cream cone, magnet, picture frame, sickle, glove, crayon, spool of thread, hot dog, comb, heart, ladder, open book, fish, pitchfork

77: clam, squirrel, shark, rabbit, mushroom, lollipop, toothbrush, shoe, flamingo's head, fish

78: mouse, crane, alligator, shark, horse, ice-cream cone, cat, toy car, sewing needle, clothespin, butterfly, sock, hat, bird, sailboat, boot, saltshaker

79: balloon, mouse, sock, artist's paintbrush, toothbrush, heart, slice of bread, hat, slipper, chipmunk, bird, bow, high-heeled shoe

80: bird, seal, turnip, turtle, spoon, screwdriver, bat, ladder, open book, pencil, top hat, flamingo, pickax, cat's head, giraffe, fish, owl, the letters **V** and **H**, two cherries

81: comb, nail, artist's paintbrush, book, pennant, hoe, toy truck, piece of cake, toothbrush, three-leaf clover, key, banana, saltshaker, cup, pliers, safety pin

82: ladle, boomerang, paintbrush, telephone receiver, sailboat, boot, mitten, ice-cream cone, bow, hammer, piece of pie, hockey stick, open book

83: ladder, book, nail, trowel, paintbrush, ring, mitten, toothbrush, tire pump, key, golf club, paper clip

84: ring, telescope, slipper, spool of thread, wrench, scissors, ice-cream pop, television set, bell, teacup, envelope, light bulb, two toothbrushes

85: a mouse, padlock, teacup, spoon, seal, candle, dog's head, slipper, dinosaur's head, heart, two birds

86-87: trowel, sailboat, rabbit, pine tree, bull's head, fork, hammer, teapot, lizard, shark, slipper, comb, horse's head, telephone receiver, fish, candle, carrot, can, tooth, toucan's head, fox's head, teacup, needle and thread, paper bag, ring, toothbrush, snail, spoon, pencil, button

88: coffeepot, funnel, toothbrush, ice-cream cone, scrub brush, iron, jar, cup and saucer, piece of cake, teapot, bell, flashlight

89: hat, puzzle piece, mug, bat, comb, campfire, boot, tied bandanna, bird, sheriff's badge

90: barbell, trowel, bowling pin, hat, sailing ship, hatchet, fish, toy car, sea gull, sailboat, lemon, bird

91: coin, hat, snail, ear of corn, pliers, fish, snake, boot, eagle's head, dove, telescope, handbell, mushroom, heart, toothbrush, cap, glass

92: fishing pole, recorder, bottle, telephone receiver, knitted hat, light bulb, teacup, snail, ladder, toothbrush, tomato, butter knife

93: stalk of broccoli, wedding ring, apple, tape measure, hairbrush, stocking, rabbit's head, bird, feather, banjo, toothbrush, boot, fish, vulture, ladder

94: pencil, closed umbrella, metal nut, bowl, nail, squirrel, lizard, iron, mouse, frog, hammer, fork, teacup, penguin

95: fish, shoe, duck, closed umbrella, butterfly, boot, envelope, rabbit, car, bird, dog, fox, ladle, pig, carrot, turtle

96: carrot, wristwatch, artist's paintbrush, toothbrush, pear, sock, telephone receiver, flashlight, key, mallet, pencil, comb, cap

97: rabbit, iron, sewing needle, toothbrush, fish, pear, ice-cream cone, telescope, button, scissors, duck, cane

98: hairbrush, comb, pencil, mug, spool of thread, pillow, pinwheel, banana, baseball cap, loaf of bread, ruler, clothespin, bottle, fish, bird, two soda cans

99: key, book, teapot, jar, piece of cake, rabbit, teacup, top hat, apple core, mouse, pocket watch, crown

100: jump rope, mouse, butterfly, baseball, comb, slipper, dolphin, fish, sailboat, ruler, flashlight, pear, duck

101: pot, feather, piece of pie, saw, butterfly, owl, wishbone, snake, pickax, carrot, bird, canoe, pencil

102: duck, golf club, flashlight, piece of cake, hat, screwdriver, seal, sock, spoon, slipper, rolling pin, nail

103: hat, pen in inkwell, horn, key, swan, hourglass, ladle, owl, eyeglasses, trowel, starfish, slice of watermelon, teacup

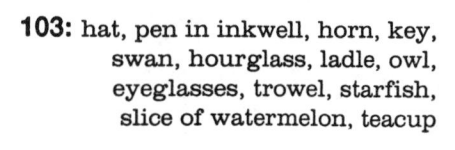

104: pot, sewing needle, ring, safety pin, balloon, whale, shoe, nail, goose, teacup, mushroom, slice of lemon, butter knife

105: baseball bat, dinosaur, ice-cream cone, life preserver, dog's head, shark, book, olive, banana, fish, boy's head, rabbit's head, nutcracker, light bulb, two birds

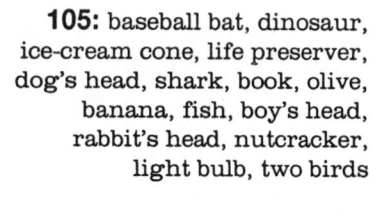

106: teakettle, paper clip, iron, boot, party hat, sock, toothbrush, pear, pencil, fishhook, spoon, ice-cream cone, plunger, nail

107: frying pan, loaf of bread, worm, bow, spool of thread, bird, ice-cream cone, padlock, paper cup, sock, piece of pie, ax, handbell, peanut

108: butterfly, mitten, feather, shark, bird, mallet, hummingbird, magnet, cat, starfish, arrowhead

109: fifteen carrots

110-111: rake, loaf of bread, owl, horse's head, rabbit, ant, penguin, piece of pie, hammer, rooster, spoon, witch's head, seashell, sailboat, fish, mouse, raccoon, lizard, fork, candle, knight's helmet, bird, gorilla's head, hat, snake, walrus's head, lion's head, seal, dog's head, eagle

112: fork, artist's paintbrush, whale, mallet, ruler, mouse, banana, penguin, pencil, apple, cowboy boot, toothbrush, coin

113: snail, bug, shark, slice of bread, peeled banana, fish, seashell, cat's head, rabbit's head, turtle, tube of paint, ice-cream cone, crab, mushroom, whale, candle, screwdriver, bee, spoon

114: book, jar, baseball cap, teacup, mitten, paintbrush, magnifying glass, toothbrush, piece of pie, bell, slipper, pencil

184

115: bell, fish, telephone receiver, whale, vase, dwarf's head, paintbrush, banana, adhesive bandage, megaphone, golf club, slice of bread, comb, book, teacup

116: dog's head, chicken, mouse, alligator's head, feather, toothbrush, mushroom, dog, bird, pear, slipper, two fish

117: pitcher, mouse, turkey, fish, carrot, loaf of bread, mitten, shoe, feather, cat, ice skate, rabbit's head, belt

118: seal, hat, shoe, piece of pie, sewing needle, screwdriver, book, lollipop, ladder, baseball bat, ice-cream cone, lamp, lamb, pennant, exclamation point, letters **B** and **E**, number 4

119: duck, butter knife, fish, piece of pie, mouse, purse, book, hat, sewing needle, light bulb, pencil, pear, artist's paintbrush, bird, rabbit, two cherries

120: fish, buffalo, butterfly, sheep, deer, mouse, rabbit, turtle, eagle, goose, bird, squirrel

121: rabbit, ice-cream cone, turtle, sailboat, scissors, baseball cap, fish, duck, snake, dog's head, comb, caterpillar, teacup, football, bell

122: baseball cap, open book, saltshaker, egg, hammer, pumpkin, mask, pear, carrot, fish, canoe, ladle, boot

123: coffeepot, nail, open umbrella, ladle, shoe, hat, crayon, orange, ring, baseball, canoe, kite, golf club

124: hot-air balloon, birdhouse, plunger, pinwheel, pocket watch, boy's head, handbell, dog, peach, carrot, scissors, tepee

125: boy's face, baseball, ice-cream cone, sock, pear, glove, fish, mouse, turtle, snake, hat, bird, eyeglasses, bell

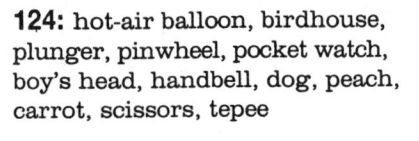

126: fan, mitten, fork, parrot, spoon, pencil, apple, nail, two socks, three mice

127: cow, fish, dinosaur, funnel, golf club, duck, cat, spoon, hammer, saltshaker, frog, carrot, chick, clothespin

128: thirteen lambs

129: crayon, sheep's head, book, mouse's head, pitcher, duck, flute, cat, steer's head, seahorse, wishbone, apple core, fox, turtle, teacup

130: scarf, snake, fish, heart, button, mouse, spoon, balloon, bird, sewing needle, two artist's paintbrushes

131: pencil, scissors, rabbit's head, baseball cap, closed umbrella, slice of pizza, frying pan, safety pin, shark, sewing needle, banana, snail, number 4, candle

132: bear, bird, golf club, rabbit, piece of pie, shovel, screwdriver, pliers, alligator, sewing needle, artist's paintbrush, key, boot, pitcher

133: shark, rabbit, fish, lizard, mouse, pencil, butterfly, seahorse, spoon, seal, snake, bird, bat

134: teapot, horn, flashlight, kite, banana, fish, bird, pencil, toothbrush, spoon, ring, teacup, turtle, cat, king's head, scissors, duck

135: duck, boot, mitten, pliers, sock, artist's paintbrush, cat, mouse, spoon, ear of corn, fishhook, flying insect, ladle, heart, sewing needle, star, two fish

136: nineteen cats

137: hamburger, shovel, scissors, teacup, ring, lollipop, saltshaker, fountain pen, skateboard, acorn, crayon

138: balloon, glove, present, ice-cream cone, safety pin, rabbit, wrapped piece of candy, dog's head, spoon, duck, eyeglasses, paper cup, banana, sock, potato

139: pennant, purse, fishing pole, acorn, artist's paintbrush, dragonfly, toothbrush, sailboat, rooster, butterfly, fish, hat, trowel, heart, bird, crescent moon, mushroom

140: mouse, alligator, canoe, snake, bonnet, cat, chicken, teacup, boomerang, dog's head, bowl, cane, spatula, shoe

141: crayon, fish, muffin, oar, ice-cream pop, sailboat, kite, rabbit, key, banana, artist's paintbrush, slipper, trowel, duck

142: balloon, book, bell, bread, barn, bee, bunny, butterfly, bird, bat, banana, brush, baseball, boat, baseball bat

143: cat, piece of pie, horse, open umbrella, carrot, mallet, mouse, bird, snake, comb, spoon, saltshaker, wishbone, snail, artist's paintbrush, chicken

144: magnet, sock, eyeglasses, whale, comb, in-line skate, book, button, bell, star, mitten, knitted hat, shoe

145: whale, rabbit, ruler, open book, mug, platter, dog's head, spatula, lizard, spoon, fish, artist's paintbrush, gorilla's head, pencil

146: mouse, open umbrella, eyeglasses, gingerbread boy, baseball bat, thong sandal, hat, teacup, cupcake, spoon, pencil, saltshaker, chef's head, mallet, sock, cat's head

147: screwdriver, envelope, coin, sock, padlock, mallet, eyeglasses, butterfly, slice of bread, book, ice-cream cone, nail

148: dolphin, ice-cream cone, boot, hummingbird, bird, light bulb, open umbrella, strawberry, pear, hat, goose, lemon wedge, pine tree, deer's head, seal's head, bell, mouse

149: lima bean, ax, ice-cream cone, kite, arrow, toothbrush, tack, flowerpot, ladle, piece of cake, pencil, spool of thread, sailboat, hoe, crown, sewing needle, heart, artist's paintbrush, recorder, bell

150: comb, spoon, artist's paintbrush, fox's head, ice-cream cone, squirrel, hawk, teacup, glove, banana, eyeglasses, chicken's head

151: horse, mushroom, toothbrush, whale, pea pod, hat, boot, cat, bone, lemon wedge, duck, flashlight, thimble, fork, nutcracker, ceramic jar, candle

152: banana, pair of dice, belt, rabbit, padlock, seal, baseball, pencil, heart, crayon, turtle, apple, two doughnuts

153: key, coat hanger, pear, golf club, tack, mug, fish, ice pop, ring, carrot, broom, pencil, book

154: wristwatch, spoon, screwdriver, cap, jump rope, comb, cowboy hat, coin, hummingbird, pencil, T-shirt, pinwheel, tent, rake

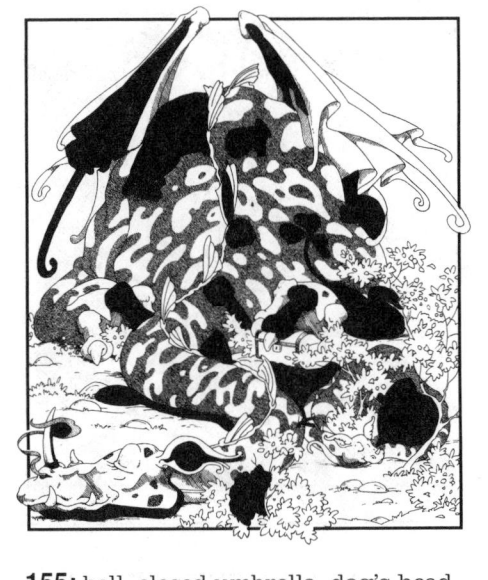

155: bell, closed umbrella, dog's head, vase, fish, musical note, tweezers, bird, rabbit's head, spoon, bone, mitten, three-leaf clover, butterfly, snake, swan, cat, key, beet

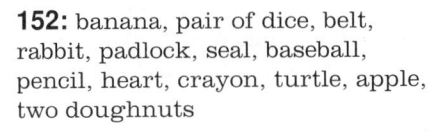

156: goose, lizard, spoon, dress, eyeglasses, open book, eagle's head, high-heeled shoe, clown's head, toucan, penguin, snail, banana, dog, heart, ring

157: saw, spider, goose, antelope, pea pod, sheep, carrot, egg, beaver, ladybug, rabbit, mouse, elephant, banana

158: spatula, crab, acorn, arrow, spool of thread, cap, sailboat, letter **A**, shoe, clam shell, parrot, pliers, cat, bird, piece of pie, ice-cream cone, tube of toothpaste

159: mitten, spoon, key, mug, shoe, magnifying glass, book, acorn, hairbrush, wrench, pencil, spatula

160: bird, open book, swan, carrot, banana, bell, pear, horse, dragonfly, envelope, butterfly, crown, cake, fork, dog

161: turtle, derby hat, pencil, bonnet, ruler, acorn, envelope, clown's head, turkey, jump rope, adhesive bandage, elephant's head, wrapped piece of candy, bird

162: carrot, penguin, snail, hot-air balloon, open umbrella, sock, key on a key ring, accordion, pine tree, coat hanger, number 7, wishbone, feather, cotton candy, diamond ring

163: nail, artist's paintbrush, fish, piece of cake, toothbrush, shoe, screwdriver, cupcake, mouse, chicken drumstick, peeled banana, pliers, hammer

164: golf club, cat, trowel, letter **A**, hammer, ice-cream cone, banana, mug, sailboat, turtle, sock, toothbrush

165: fish, dog's head, canoe, bird, crescent moon, coat hanger, artist's paintbrush, dragonfly, tweezers, sailboat, mouse, flower, tube of paint, hairbrush, bee, butterfly, comb

166: rabbit, sock, fish, teacup, light bulb, artist's paintbrush, pillow, teddy bear, handbell, Santa's hat, hammer, spoon, carrot, shovel, toothbrush

167: book, camera, key, iron, sewing needle, apple core, saw, lizard, hairbrush, pennant, paper clip, tube of toothpaste, two birds